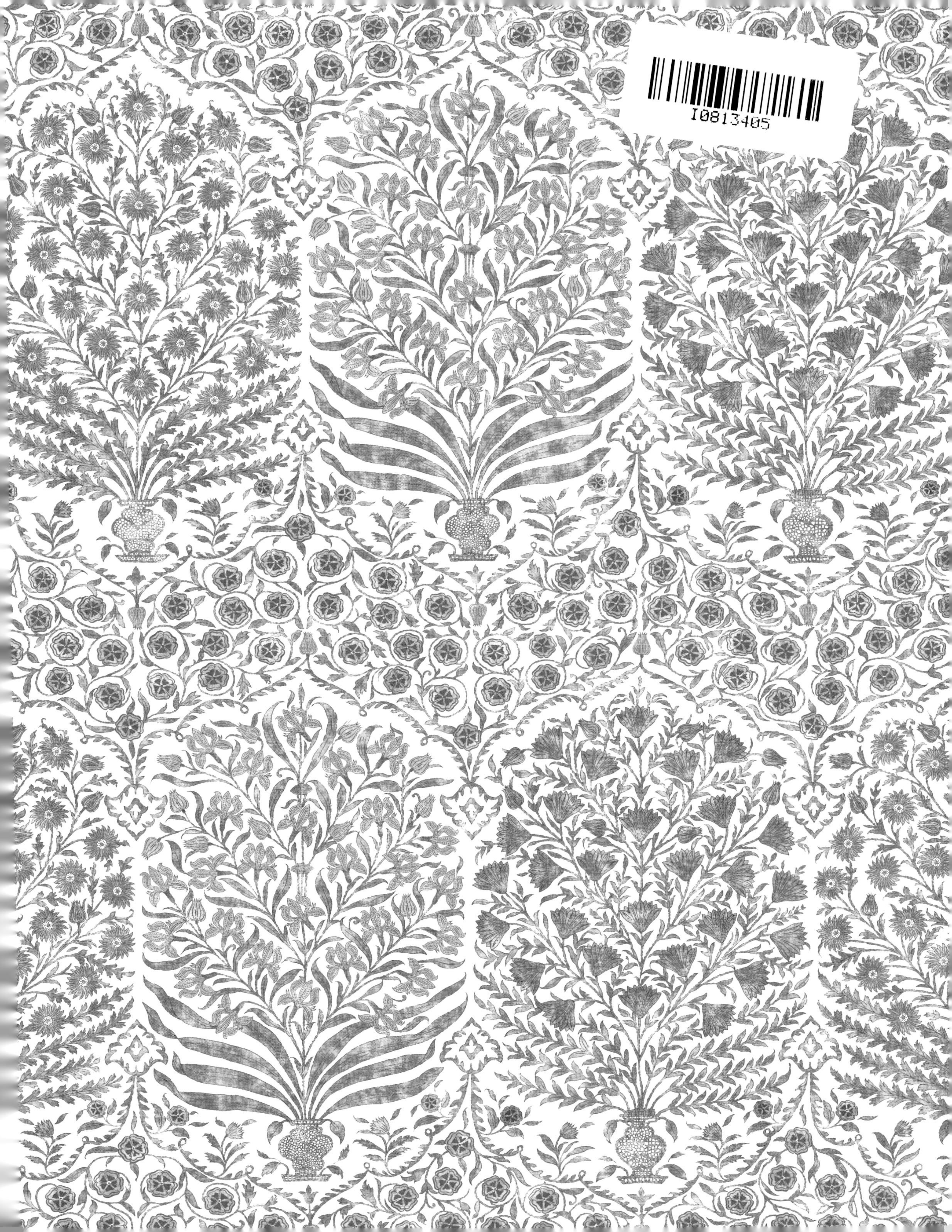
I0813405

THE HAPPY HOME

THE HAPPY HOME

LAYERED INTERIORS FOR JOYFUL LIVING

ARIEL OKIN

FOREWORD BY LENA DUNHAM

PRINCIPAL PHOTOGRAPHY BY DONNA DOTAN

RIZZOLI
NEW YORK
New York · Paris · London · Milan

For Ben, whose boundless love and pure goodness never cease to amaze me.
I'm the luckiest in the whole world that you're mine. And for
S + A — being your mommy is the greatest gift I could ever dream of.
I love you more!

For my mom, whose joy, style, and all-encompassing warmth inspire me every day.
And for my dad, whose love of learning and appreciation for nature are a part of me.

And for Bubby, who is absolutely one of a kind.
Thank you for instilling your knack for storytelling in me.

CONTENTS

FOREWORD
BY LENA DUNHAM

At its best, decor is personal—it says something not just about what its inhabitants own but about who they are, what they value, and the things that make them feel safe. Yet so much interior design is the antithesis of this—anesthetized modern spaces, all sharp corners and pale shades, creating a void where there should be warmth and love. Books by the foot, impractical objects, and fleeting trends fill so many design magazines and blogs.

But Ariel Okin's work is the opposite of everything we've come to expect from the interiors of the Internet. She revels in softness, specificity, and livability, while consistently surprising with her choices. I've been lucky enough to work with her on two homes—each time I was at a crossroads in my life, needing what only a real home can provide. I had always been cautious about working with a designer on something as personal as my living space, but when Ariel appeared it was clear that her instincts combined an almost maternal coziness with the inventive specificity that only an artist can bring. She bathed the first house in unexpected color (dusty pink and deepest blue-green), as well as whimsy (a watercolor lamp shade covered in dancing legs, another in octopi). She found pieces that felt both well-loved and totally fresh, surprising yet familiar.

When it was time for her to tackle my next space, I was awed by the fact that she didn't try and recreate the earlier home, or any of her other projects—each of which feels like it has her calling card but is also faithful not just to the personality of the resident but to the personality of the home itself. She leans into architectural details, embraces flaws, and stays alive with unique references that call back periods from Art Deco to Victorian, from 1990s minimalism to 1970s freedom. She reminds me that our homes are the most personal expressions we have, the places where our dreams can go wild. As a writer, I have to look

around and sense a world that is as expansive as it is private. Ariel gives me that.

So peruse this book, and then peruse it again, to get the kinds of ideas that will make you look at your space in a new way. Whether it's a studio or a mansion, one bedroom or ten, Ariel treats every space with love and will remind you that no home is ever too small, or too dark, or too cramped—and it is never too late—for you to surround yourself with everyday beauty.

ABOVE: Lena Dunham's West Village apartment, featured on the cover of the fall 2019 issue of *Domino*. The carpet is Pierre Frey, and the cushions are from Dedar Milano.

INTRODUCTION

I became an interior designer by accident. As a kid, I loved to read and write; my nose was always in a book. My mom would take me to the local Barnes & Noble to browse and relax after school, and the arts and interiors section became my happy place. I vividly remember poring over Slim Aarons anthologies with a snack in hand, enraptured by the transportive bright swathes of color and detail. Those moments spent at the bookstore with my mother marked the beginning of my love affair with interiors, but it took many years for me to realize that something I found so beautiful and interesting could also become a career.

When I was twelve, my parents built a home just down the road from where we were living, on the Main Line in the suburbs of Philadelphia. They both have sharp eyes for detail and truly enjoy the architecture and design process, and the home was inspired by the historic old Pennsylvania stone field houses local to the area. It had charming character and a warm, inviting atmosphere, and I was frequently brought along to the construction site visits, absorbing it like a sponge. I loved everything about being on site, from the smells of fresh paint to the impact of even the smallest decisions on the overall end-product.

My parents let me pick everything for my bedroom myself with some gentle guidance, and I still remember every square inch of not only my room, but the entire house, and how it made me feel. It was a happy home—the interiors were elegant, warm, layered, and full of life. It left a lasting imprint on me and my design DNA.

I grew up, graduated high school, and moved out of my childhood home, going on to college in Washington, D.C., where I majored in English and journalism, and then to graduate school in New York, where I studied strategic communication with a focus on public affairs. Design as a career was never on my radar. But in my spare time, any chance I got, I was immersed in interiors: poring over vintage design books, pausing the TV to study sets, getting lost in shelter magazines. My relaxation

was tied up with interiors—the subject was my happy place, just like the arts and interiors section of the bookstore was when I was a kid. And then, a funny thing started happening.

Shortly after I finished my graduate program and started my first job, friends started asking me for help with their apartments. One had just moved in with a boyfriend, another had moved into her first studio, and all made the same request: "I love what you've done with your place. Can you help me?" It seemed to come totally out of left field, but I willingly obliged, and instantly I began spending more time helping friends for free than I was spending on my actual job. Around this time, I started contributing as a writer to *Vogue*'s living section, as well as to other outlets like *Architectural Digest* and *Domino*, and my passion for interiors grew even stronger. I found the combination of designing spaces while also writing about them to be not only engaging, but also incredibly immersive and fulfilling.

Still, I was afraid of the unknown—leaving a career for something that felt like it came out of the blue, though it utterly enraptured me, seemed risky. So I juggled both jobs for years, balancing a full day of work with an evening of design client presentations, traipsing around the city with a bag full of samples stuffed underneath my laptop, all while trying to meet new editorial deadlines for the outlets I had started contributing to.

Three years later, I went out on my own full time, thanks to the encourage-

On-site during the construction of a childhood home.

ment of my husband and my mother. I had been lucky enough to have one of my projects appear in *Elle Decor*, and that feature, plus a growing presence on social media, had brought in enough work to sustain the firm, at least for a few months. I finally felt ready to take the leap. (Needless to say, I'm so glad I did!)

I realize now that the aspect I love the most about interiors isn't the shopping, or the puzzle of figuring out the floor plans (though I do love both), but the story of a home's inhabitants, and how to weave that into their surroundings in thoughtful and meaningful ways. It is an immense privilege to be able to craft the "movie sets" where my clients create their memories. Threading the needle between the people I work with, their history, and how it's reflected in their spaces is an endlessly fascinating and deeply personal process.

In the decade since I opened Ariel Okin Interiors, my team and I have worked on countless projects across the country with truly wonderful clients, many of whom I've had the pleasure of getting to know over the course of multiple projects. We've watched our clients grow their families with new additions, put down roots in towns both new and familiar, and begin fresh adventures in their spaces. I never take for granted the fact that with every project, we are being welcomed into someone's house to help them turn it into a home. Our job is to enrich these spaces, transforming each one into the client's very own happy place. We recreate the warmth, comfort, and joy that the house on Fenimore Lane brought me all those years ago.

If you take away anything from this book, I hope it's this: Don't be afraid to pursue the things that light you up, even if they come out of left field. Say yes to interests and experiences that bring you joy, even if you don't know where they may lead. They just might help you create your own happy place, however that may look.

I am eternally grateful that you have chosen to read this book, a chronicling of the first ten years of my firm's work. Every home I design is fully inspired by its owners—and I hope you find some inspiration from them, and us, along the way.

Warmly,
Ariel Okin

JOSEPH DIRAND Interior
Hadley Keller
POOLSIDE

PLAYFUL MEETS POLISHED

On my first call with potential new clients in Greenwich, Connecticut, I was told right off the bat that this husband and wife had very different styles and that merging their two aesthetics would be the main task at hand. The design prompt: mixing the husband's preppy/polished sensibilities with the wife's funky, bohemian aesthetic. He works in finance and likes tweeds and tartans with an East Coast, practical sensibility; she is a warm, bubbly fashion designer from Brazil who loves color and pattern.

A home is more than just a collection of objects; it's the feeling those items evoke. In this house, cheerful energy rules the roost.

The pair had just relocated to Greenwich from the suburbs of Detroit with four children and three dogs in tow, and they wanted to settle into their forever home. They came with an abundance of sports equipment, dog leashes, games, and toys, which meant there needed to be places to accommodate the accoutrements of an active life, but we also would be required to make the house feel like a home. At the same time, we were tasked with creating spaces that were elevated, grown-up, and appropriate for the owners' frequent entertaining.

We were presented with a 9,000-square-foot home in Greenwich that had been rented out for the previous ten years; it was not kept up well and was in need of a facelift. The house was a beige Tuscan remnant of the early 2000s, replete with dark granite and swooping corbels—and yet, it had good bones. The clients trusted our opinion about what needed to be changed to realize their vision, and in addition to starting from scratch with the decorating, we landed on a light gut.

OPPOSITE: A welcoming entry is conjured with warm wood, a custom marigold Greek key dhurrie stair runner made in England, an antique entry hall table, and a hand-thrown lamp in a verdigris finish. FOLLOWING PAGES: A crisp and airy formal living room feels inviting and mixes the clients' own antique case piece at left with custom upholstery and warm marigold and emerald-green textiles to contrast with the creamy base palette. A hand-lacquered ceiling draws the eye up and makes the ceilings feel taller while reflecting light across the room.

RICHARD
DIEBENKORN
MISSONI
HYDRANGEAS
HINCKLEY YACHTS

SLIM AARONS

A NOTE ON ENTRYWAYS

- Pair patinated pieces with modern silhouettes to create beautiful tension.
- Allot specific areas for fresh flowers, books, and accessories to add in layers
- Start with function: make note of what kind of storage is needed (i.e., for keys and mail) and work it into your furniture plan.
- Weave colors from the palette into the accessories: book spines, boxes, lampshades, and trays, for example, can tie a space together.

ABOVE: A custom dhurrie in marigold, cream, and emerald provides personality. BOTTOM LEFT: A vintage painted faux-tortoise coffee table in the formal living room adds texture and charm. OPPOSITE: A gilded vintage sunburst mirror opens up the foyer by bouncing light off the set of double doors opposite the front door. FOLLOWING PAGES: The living room is anchored by the clients' vintage case piece, peeling with age and patina and filled with treasures like vintage French Aptware. The green chinoiserie screen was found at a local thrift shop in Greenwich and served as the inspiration for the palette. Vintage architectural prints lend a sense of gravitas to balance the chintz florals.

JULIAN SCHNABEL

CHANEL
LITCHFIELD STYLE
MYSTIQUE
SLIM AARONS WOMEN
BEACHSIDE
WINDSOR

What did that mean? While the footprint remained the same, everything within it changed. We began by sanding down the dated orange floors and restaining them a dark and rich walnut to evoke the heritage feeling of a house that had been there much longer than it had. The kitchen is always the heart of the home, but that is especially true in a house with four teenagers and three dogs. We reconsidered the space both aesthetically and functionally. We stripped the walls of a dingy sand-hued wallpaper, repainted the millwork in a warm, inviting white, and rebuilt the kitchen island to better accommodate the specific appliances and entertaining needs of the family. We also updated the decorative elements (e.g., lighting and hardware) to bring them in line with the house's new aesthetic. The bathrooms all received a slight upgrade: fresh paint, wallpaper, and new hardware, fittings, and fixtures.

The decorating was wholly influenced by the family's personality and history, as well as their need to have a home that was casual and proper at the same time. Ebullient monkeys grace the less formal powder room used by the children off the mudroom, while a more elegant palm tree motif ensconces the formal powder room. The dining room mural by Iksel is a panorama of Brazil, the wife's home country. And classic, tailored, polished silhouettes, like English roll arm sofas, English and American antiques, and sisal carpeting, ground the house in the sort of smart comfort favored by the husband. The tension of playful meets polished is at the core of this house.

The pièce de résistance? A scroll artwork depicting beautiful sea coral and moss, found tucked in the back of the clients' basement

A NOTE ON POWDER ROOMS

- Powder rooms have different functions depending on location. Formal powder rooms should feel elevated and transportive, while back-of-house bathrooms need to be functional for everyday use without sacrificing charm.
- Consider painting the vanity and/or millwork a unique color to tie into the wallpaper, or the palette in adjoining rooms.
- A powder room offers an opportunity to have fun—treat it like a jewel box with a lacquered ceiling or vanity, uniquely patterned wallpaper, or interesting lighting and mirror details.

PREVIOUS PAGES: A Brazilian landscape mural by Iksel reminds the wife of her home country; hand-painted tenting on the ceiling injects whimsy into an otherwise formal space. A custom rug offers contrast with a chocolate geometric border. ABOVE AND RIGHT: We wanted to evoke the clients' personalities by leaning into color and pattern via the vanities and wallpaper in these powder rooms.

OPPOSITE AND ABOVE: The kitchen was reworked to be more functional by adding a large island that serves as a gathering space and the ideal place for a buffet. We kept it classic with creamy white cabinetry, unlacquered brass that will age beautifully over time, and fresh green tones to draw in the view from the window over the main sink. In my opinion, white kitchens are timeless.

THIS PAGE AND OPPOSITE: The breakfast nook serves many purposes, chief among them working as a spot for casual dining and homework. We liked the fact that the vintage table had lived a life already; it didn't matter if pen ink got etched into it by accident. The array of geometric textiles on the bench cushions are a nice foil to the sinuous palm artwork. The mirrored sconces on the wall (opposite) were a previously unused engagement gift to the couple that we pulled out of storage.

ABOVE AND OPPOSITE: The coral scroll artwork above the fireplace inspired the color story in the family room. A variety of textiles combine with pea-green grasscloth to create a vibrant palette. Multiple seating zones allow for multiple uses: backgammon in one corner, reading nooks in another, and a large sofa, custom-crafted for this very tall family of six to flop down on and relax.

A cheerful color palette can do wonders to set the tone for a space, allowing guests and inhabitants to feel both energized and at ease.

when we searched through what they already owned. The scroll, discovered by the wife at a flea market (she has a good eye!), became the inspiration for the color palette of the family room off the kitchen, one of the most high-traffic rooms in the house. Rich coral, toned down mossy greens, and hints of navy play together to create a space designed to be enjoyed: from a deep blue backgammon table to a sofa trimmed in cheerful marigold. The latter was custom-built to comfortably accommodate this tall family of six. Everything in this home is bespoke and intentional, so that when they walked in for the big reveal, it already fit like a glove.

This project presented a challenge of understanding who they are and what they need in order to live in their home happily—both functionally and decoratively. Throughout, each family member's interests and preferences informed the process, with a lot of fun along the way. Our clients tell us that the resulting finished product is their favorite place to be.

OPPOSITE: A quiet nook tucked away at the top of the second floor is used for doing homework, writing notes, or getting through paperwork. The palette of marigold, green, chocolate brown, and neutrals continues with a plush Stark carpet that feels nice underfoot, trimmed in a yellow cotton binding that echoes the front foyer stair runner. Woven wood roman blinds add texture. FOLLOWING PAGES: In this mudroom, we added custom lockers with name tags for each of the four children to keep sports equipment, backpacks, and coats tidy and tucked away. The green tassels were added so that the youngest—not yet tall enough yet to reach the knob—could open his locker himself, while tying the color palette together with the vintage cabbage plates on the wall.

A NOTE ON MUDROOMS

- A mudroom sits at the intersection of form and function. Often a main entry point to the home, it needs to feel considered without being precious.
- Flooring should be durable, but can still be cheerful, like this black and white checkered tile.
- Seating is nice if you have room; everyone appreciates a place to perch while putting on shoes. Ample hanging space for coats is always welcomed, bonus points if you can conceal the mess behind doors, like we did with the custom lockers in this mudroom.
- Wainscoting or beadboard adds architecture and is easy to clean.

PREVIOUS PAGES: We were inspired by the beautiful bedroom at Tory Burch's Southampton estate for this primary bedroom. Vintage Greek key nightstands contrast with powder-blue Christopher Spitzmiller lamps, and a custom skirted table hides secret storage. ABOVE AND OPPOSITE: The chintz floral is the star of the show. Nobilis faux bois wallpaper ensconces the bedroom in peaceful energy. FOLLOWING PAGES: We made this teen boy's room elevated and cool.

A NOTE ON CHILDREN'S BEDROOMS

- Children's rooms should grow with them; punch up the sophistication.
- A solid-colored, textured paper in a performance material is a great starting point: it can work from nursery to teen.
- Artwork doesn't have to be cutesy: a framed map of the world or a print of the solar system can add color without being over the top.
- The sky's the limit: add unexpected details in places like lampshades, ceilings (Mario Buatta famously called them the fifth wall for this reason), and bedding.

THE WORLD

PREVIOUS PAGES: Playful elements, like the embroidered stars on the wallpaper and the sweet gingham roman shades, evoke the fun of childhood without feeling too childish. OPPOSITE: A versatile outdoor space flexes as a pretty bar for entertaining. ABOVE: The pool is styled with loungers and umbrellas in hunter green, white, and iron, highlighting the surrounding natural palette. Durable materials like stone and iron make for elegant outdoor furniture that could live just as nicely indoors as it does outside.

A FAMILY GROWS IN BROOKLYN

I love when clients aren't afraid of color. This family had recently purchased a historic townhouse in Park Slope and had been living in it for a few months without touching the interiors. They were craving jewel tones and saturated hues to bring energy and liveliness to their new home, and they wanted the space to reflect the full and modern life of two busy working parents with a two-year-old son and a baby girl on the way.

This classic Park Slope townhouse, built in 1901, was beautifully restored by a contracting team before the clients purchased it, but many aspects still felt builder-grade bland. The kitchen needed a redo, as did the bathrooms; the paint colors were

Plums, neutrals, and greens play nicely together in this Park Slope living room. The original stained-glass windows (circa 1901) were an important detail for us to preserve and highlight. An oversized cerused French mirror hangs above the original fireplace mantel and bounces natural light from the bay windows. Textured finishes like plaster and verdigris add a handmade, human touch.

Functionality is the main spoke on a design wheel: every home has to make sense for how its inhabitants live.

a wan gray across the board. One of our directives was to inject color, and lots of it, so we searched for the most interesting hues we could find: deep plums reminiscent of summer eggplant paired with patinated verdigris for the formal living space; an orangey-yellow lacquer, sunshiny yet rich, like a perfect egg yolk, paired with a beautifully veined honed Italian marble for the wet bar in the family area; sage green Zellige tiles, worn and lived-in, for the upstairs bathrooms.

But the most important directive in this project was to pair function with form: make it beautiful, yes, but, crucially, make it work for the way they live. When they first moved into the house, they weren't entertaining much because the formal living room felt cut off from the dining area, and the kitchen didn't offer a place to hang out or watch TV in a more casual setting. There was no playroom for the kids, no guest room for grandparents or friends to sleep over. The primary bathroom shower didn't work, and many of the rooms were simply painted white with no furniture in them, waiting for us to assign them meaning (and spice them up).

OPPOSITE: Camel tufted leather, aging nicely in the sun, contrasts beautifully with the deep plums and aubergines of the textiles. Artwork by Dawn Michelle Wolfe pulls the palette together. The woven cabinet mimics the weave on the sisal carpeting, and the upholstered iron chairs have a small-scale geometric pattern that brings in just the tiniest hint of yellow.
FOLLOWING PAGES: The formal dining room twinkles with sophisticated personality, anchored by a set of Art Deco Italian chairs we reupholstered in a pale-blue Schumacher vegan performance leather. This proper dining area allows the clients to entertain as they had always envisioned. The table is from Bunny Williams Home. The original door from 1901.

A NOTE ON WORKING WITH HISTORIC HOMES

- Try to preserve original millwork, doors, and windows as much as possible. If an item isn't working in a particular space, see how it can be salvaged for another area of the home.
- Incorporate silhouettes that feel appropriate to the period when the house was built, without turning it into a time capsule.
- Mix and match furniture eras for a collected look that still nods to the past.

LEFT: A saturated, gorgeous yellow by Farrow & Ball—appropriately called Orangery—used on the cabinetry is the anchor for this wet bar that ties the kitchen into the family room. We paired it with a beautifully veined honed Italian marble and unlacquered brass fittings for a chic spot for cocktails or coffee. OPPOSITE: The family room invites with a custom green velvet mohair sectional and a clever storage ottoman for toys.

Our initial goal was to listen, which we did, and based on what we heard we figured out what this family needed from the house: a flex play space with a good pull-out sofa so that it could turn into a guest bedroom on a whim; a primary bedroom that would serve as a relaxing retreat from hectic work schedules; and a dream patio added to the back of the house. These changes made the house feel not only like a home, but like their home.

One of the first things we did was to cohesively link the long galley-like rectangular space that runs from the front to the back of the house. This kind of space is typical of brownstone layouts, and it can be tricky for space planning. Often the formal living area bleeds into the dining room, kitchen, and family room without clear delineation. We wanted to provide soft structure to the rectangular layout

ABOVE: Antiqued glass and Farrow & Ball's Stiffkey Blue in high gloss pair with unlacquered brass fittings for a sexy, moody bar on the ground level of this townhouse. OPPOSITE: The color story continues into the snug, where a game table sits next to the bar for whiskey and backgammon.

The rusty mohair velvet on the couch was the basis for this cozy TV room. It's offset by an inky navy textured wallpaper; warm reds and marigold sing in contrast. Burl and camel leather add a masculine touch, and a plush wool herringbone carpet in a smart camel lies underfoot.

Homer Remington
Soul of a Nation

PREVIOUS PAGES: The kitchen palette and textiles were inspired by the colors in the original stained glass windows. RIGHT: The primary bedroom is a soothing respite from the business of the world, yet still feels playful and happy because it incorporates spicy colors in small doses. Artwork over the bed was commissioned from Dawn Michelle Wolfe.

ABOVE: We retained the primary bedroom's original plasterwork panels, trimming the silk wallpaper to go around those zones. The desk offers a quiet place to work. OPPOSITE: Hints of plum (on the window treatment's leading edge) and marigold tie the downstairs to the upstairs.

A NOTE ON MULTIPURPOSE SPACES

- Spaces that grown-ups inhabit don't have to be serious: playful can work for all ages.
- For spaces used by the whole family, try a pattern that's fun without reading strictly kid-centric, like the large-scale polka dot we used in the playroom-turned-guest room, opposite.
- Think about how both adults and kids will be utilizing and interacting with a space when conjuring a floor plan. Consider, for example, where adults will sit and where kids will play.

ABOVE AND LEFT: The son's bedroom also serves as a play space, as many city kid bedrooms do, so we left ample floor space for imaginative play, while also designing a reading nook with a comfy chair that can fit both a grown-up and a child, book storage, and a side table for a small lamp and a glass of water. OPPOSITE: This children's playroom on the ground floor serves double duty as a guest bedroom when family visits from out of town.

City spaces can feel just as warm and inviting as country retreats. Engaging with the outdoors adds a dynamic sense of beauty.

to allow for front-of-house formal entertaining spaces and everyday high-traffic spaces toward the back, without adding walls or having one area say more than the others.

We accomplished this by utilizing rugs as markers for different zones, including the living and dining areas. We also crafted a custom sofa to fit into a little nook tucked across from the kitchen to give them a proper family room where they had just empty space before. We boarded up a nonworking fireplace at the back of the kitchen to make way for a built-in banquette, table, and dining chairs and extended the island for more seating and prep space. Their family of four now enjoys pancake breakfasts in a true eat-in kitchen.

The best compliment we received when it was all finished? That the renovation helped our clients use the house the way they wanted to. While previously the thought of throwing a dinner party caused confusion (where would they sit?), now an elegant flow from cocktails in the living room to dinner at the table provides structure. The rooms are multifunctional and personal—there to support them as they grow and thrive in their dynamic new space.

OPPOSITE: A new deck off the primary bedroom set the stage to fulfill a longstanding dream for the clients: morning coffee outside, among the trees. Simple iron outdoor furniture with white upholstery feels crisp and clean against blue-and-white geometric pillows. Planters of various heights add to the feeling of a townhouse in the sky.

BEACHSIDE CHIC

Each type of home has its own "secret ingredient," and for beach homes in particular, the special sauce is usually a large dose of fun. A quirky dash of whimsy, whether in the form of cheeky color palettes, irreverent artwork, or bold, funky textile patterns, helps to add personality to second homes, while creating an engaging, interesting and lively backdrop for happy summer memories.

This client and her husband were native Upper East Siders with three sons in their teens and early twenties. They envisioned the ultimate summer entertaining house, but one that was also functional

A beach house is meant to be fun. It shouldn't take itself too seriously, and it should push the envelope creatively. If not there, where?

for the occasional off-season visit. Our task was to realize their wishes in time for the upcoming season. We had just six months—which would make it the firm's quickest turnaround ever—but somehow we made it happen!

Situated on a leafy lot within walking distance of Main Street, with a pea gravel driveway that delightfully crunches underfoot and buffered by gorgeous plantings and a serene pool, the historic white-clapboard farmhouse had an interesting history. Just a few years prior, it had been renovated and moved to its current location, where it was used as a designer show house. Every room had a dizzying array of wallpaper with disparate finishes, and the directive was to strip it back into a cohesive, fun, layered family home with nods to its historic roots.

The clients got the house back to neutral, quite literally, once they started the renovation process. When they removed the show-house finishes, it became a blank slate—and it needed an injection of personality and charm. Our client gravitated to funky, layered eclecticism anchored by an edge of modernism. She is a collector in the truest sense

OPPOSITE: A welcoming entry, fit for the beach. The unfussy, natural fiber and casual cotton dhurrie rugs are perfect for inevitably sandy feet. Cheerful oversized Talavera plates from Casa Gusto and punchy pillows—including one in a citrus Libertine for Schumacher print—add a graphic pop, while a handmade shell mirror and green and white striped lampshade provide beachy kitsch.

PASSIONS in PRINT
Vivan Sundaram
PRESTEL

Murals are one of the most transformative tricks in design. Use them to create a magical sense of ambiance, adding a "wow factor" for both guests and residents alike.

PREVIOUS PAGES: A celestial Schumacher toile brings swathes of pattern to the ceiling, while the hand-embroidered blue-and-white textile on the window treatments adds three dimensionality. A small pop of coral offsets the Delft color palette. RIGHT: The client fell in love with this mural the first time we showed it to her. The weeping willow is the star of the dining room.

M/S MARY
QUEEN
OF PEACE
MANILA
Photo: Grannis
POOLS

OF PEACE
MANILA
S.S MARY
QUEEN
OYSTER
EXTRAORDINARY INTERIORS

M/S MARY
QUEEN
OF PEACE
MANILA
OYSTER

Wherever a home is situated, lean into local influences to impart a sense of place.

of the word, and had a vast array of unique artwork to play with, which helped to inform the palette early on.

In the joint kitchen/breakfast/family room, we started with a pair of beautifully framed bright orange life preservers. The client had bought them at auction at Doyle years prior but didn't know what to do with them. We decided to hang them in a prime spot on the wall in the family room; not only were they a great conversation starter, they also inspired the palette for the room. We liked the nod to the beach that they brought, and their vivid hue can be found bouncing around the side chairs, kitchen counter stools, and lampshades, while soothing cool-toned light blues and natural-woods act as a visual counterweight, subtly echoing the sand and sea.

In the game room, a space where the whole family convenes to watch movies or sit by the fire on a rainy day and complete a puzzle, we proposed a celestial-themed navy and white wallpaper to apply to the coffered ceiling—a pattern with personality in spades. And in the primary bedroom, a glimmering

PREVIOUS PAGES: Framed orange life preservers, bought at auction at Doyle, were the starting point for this room. A neutral palette, punctuated by pops of ocean blue and coral, like the inside of a conch shell, evoke the beach. LEFT: The wicker dining chairs from Design Within Reach around the breakfast table play nicely with the custom Jeanneret-inspired armchairs in the living room.

OPPOSITE AND ABOVE: Wallpaper from my collection with The Mural Source turns this bedroom into a peaceful English garden. The pale blue Murano chandelier contrasts beautifully with the sage green in the wallpaper and on the upholstered vintage bench. A custom pale blue linen bed from Bunny Williams Home establishes a formal presence, countered by the fun faux tortoise nightstands found at KRB.

For
SALE
PIE

A NOTE ON GUEST BEDROOMS

- Guest bedrooms in vacation homes get lots of use, but not by the homeowner. Consider the overnight experience when planning how to orient the space. Night-stands with drawers and room for a carafe, dimmable lighting by the bed, a bench to lay out clothing or luggage, and a chair to read in are always welcome additions.
- Guest rooms offer an opportunity to experiment with a pattern or bold color that you might otherwise be afraid to use. Try something out of the box!
- Incorporate different patterns and colors in the bedding for an unexpected source of layering. Throws in saturated colors, printed shams—the mix makes it fun.

PREVIOUS PAGES, OPPOSITE, AND THIS PAGE: We wanted each guest bedroom to feel warm and welcoming—and distinct. In this guest room, vintage folk art (above), the client's own, injects personality and color into an otherwise calming space. A Scalamandré velvet tiger pillow—a classic pattern—adds a bit of unexpected funk to the bohemian bedding program. At right, the homeowner's collection of blue-and-white china sits pretty atop a bone inlay chest of drawers in the same palette. The textured shell mirror behind it conjures a beachy, breezy mood.

THIS PAGE AND OPPOSITE: Textured neutral grass-cloth lets the greens sing in this first-floor guest bedroom. Matouk bedding in a botanical print echoes the framed painted botanicals set in weathered oak frames against white linen mats. A neutral oversized suzani adds pattern to the bed. The roll armchair in a classic fern print offers a welcoming spot for reading. A chocolate brown lamp by Christopher Spitzmiller provides contrast to the creams and greens.

AKER
AROLYNE ROEHM

The exterior of a house tells just as much of a story as the interior. Architecture, landscape, and the siting of a house all inform a home's interior design.

pool-blue Murano chandelier looks like a sea creature who came right out of the surf a few blocks away. The client was willing to take design risks with bold choices, and this fostered a sense of fun in the house.

Durability and comfort were also constant considerations in our selections, given the client's frequent summer entertaining. Carefree functionality ran as an undercurrent beneath all of our decision-making, as evidenced by the natural fiber rugs (perfect for high-traffic areas) and spill-proof performance fabrics incorporated throughout. The multipurpose spaces are elevated enough to be worthy of a sophisticated cocktail party, and yet our client doesn't need to worry if someone spills some red wine on the carpet. The combination of irreverent design paired with a *laissez-faire* approach to the furnishings makes for the perfect beach house home: comfortable, yes, but also delightfully unexpected.

OPPOSITE: Mature grasses and landscaping by the front gate at this Southampton home feel welcoming and lush; the wraparound porch is protected by a sea of limelight hydrangeas. FOLLOWING PAGES: The front porch gets the most gorgeous slanted sunlight in the afternoon, making it an ideal napping spot.

EAST MEETS WEST

How do you combine the rustic feel of the mountains in Jackson Hole, Wyoming, with the buttoned-up vibe of the hedgerow-lined, coastal enclave of Oyster Bay? Such was the quandary we faced with this house, a renovation and decorating project for a young couple who had recently relocated from the scenic valley in the West to the Atlantic coast with their young son.

The clients are warm and unpretentious, yet worldly and sophisticated, and they wanted their house to reflect as such. What did that look like? We started with cozy, nubby neutrals combined with rich jewel tones and saturated hues, shades to which

PREVIOUS PAGES: The formal sitting room invites guests to settle down and read or play a round of backgammon. Rose Tarlow wallpaper with a quiet hand-painted stripe defines the space. OPPOSITE: The custom upholstery pairs nicely with a vintage game table from the Antique & Artisan Gallery. ABOVE: The slipper chair by the window beckons guests to sit and stay awhile, and a vintage floral textile draped on the back of the sofa brings soft peaches and blues into the mix.

Lucian Freud MONUMENTAL

Balancing light and dark color stories from room to room allows for a different experience in each space. One room can be cozy, another airy—and both provide comfort in different ways.

the wife gravitated. We added bohemian patterns like block prints, mud cloth, and relaxed stripes for a hint of the West, and then paired them with luxe velvet mohair in delicious solid shades of mink and aubergine, sage and sky blue. To give the home a preppy, Oyster Bay accent, we layered in classic American prints such as checks, tartan, and chintz.

Anthropologically blending two zones of the country with such distinct and disparate looks was a challenge, but it was a fun task. As the clients were not bringing any furniture with them from Wyoming, we had free rein to source items for the entire house at once, which made it easier to tell a consistent story. To add patina and age to an otherwise relatively new twenty-year-old home, we turned to some of our favorite antique shops in Locust Valley and Stamford, where we found treasures that injected the timeworn personality our clients were seeking.

In the dining room, we paired a set of eight vintage cerused-oak French chairs, reupholstered in a mix of solid velvet and floral chintz,

OPPOSITE: The cozy den offers darker contrast to the light and airy formal sitting room framed by the French doors. The yellow in the client's existing artwork makes the blues and greens sing. Deep emerald-green grasscloth makes the snug den feel like a jewel box.

Mixing eras in furniture and types of textiles—classic checks versus vintage embroidery—creates a collected, lived-in feeling.

with a newly commissioned dining table made in the style of a Swedish antique. The table is custom-sized to the room and includes a leaf that extends it to accommodate more guests when the clients host for the holidays. The room also features a rush bench that adds a hint of farmhouse style, bone inlay objects for some *esprit bohème*, and a large-scale piece of modern art and mochaware plates hung on the walls. It's cosmopolitan and country at the same time.

In the bedrooms, we struck a balance by deploying a mix of traditional florals knocked slightly off-kilter with interesting hues, such as burnt umber and acid green. We also used those out-of-the-box colorways to counter tailored silhouettes, so classic swivel armchairs are covered in a rust velvet, and prim-and-proper scalloped euro shams from Matouk are outlined in shocking chartreuse.

The mohair mink-brown sofa is plush and cozy for TV watching and reading. The sage green tape trim on the bottom of the sofa elaborates upon the color story with a geometric spin, and the custom kilim in green and brown ties the palette together, picking up cues from the leather upholstered ottoman. A lumbar pillow created from a yellow vintage Indian textile adds spunk.

A NOTE ON DINING ROOMS

- Dining rooms should be able to accommodate intimate gatherings and scale up to seat a dozen or more. Intended use of space, lighting, and floor plans are all important factors when thinking about a dining room.
- Let the architecture of the room guide the table shape. Round and oval tables are nice when entertaining, but sometimes a room calls for sharper lines.
- Vary the light sources in the room. Put dimmers on every fixture, including lamps, for a warm glow.
- Spare seating can flank sideboards and sit under sconces, adding different heights and allowing the eye to travel.

THIS PAGE AND OPPOSITE: We injected a bohemian sensibility into the dining room with a green chintz on the backs of vintage French chairs, and a large-scale wild plum floral on the window treatments. The dining table was made in the style of an antique Gustavian piece. The sky-blue wallpaper contrasts beautifully with the rich, dark wood of the bone inlay mirror and the bases of the hurricane lamps and eggplant hand-thrown lamps. Penny Morrison lampshades tie the color scheme together.

AMERICAN HOME
LIVING BY THE
the Library of Congress
HENRI ROUSSEAU
INTERIORS
THE MASTERWORKS
GREAT BEAR
MATISSE

PREVIOUS PAGES: The great room feels collected and airy. Block prints, stripes, and embroidered vintage textiles mingle with a pale blue-and-white cotton dhurrie rug. A rush and teak coffee table from Peter Dunham's Hollywood at Home anchors the space. ABOVE: Mochaware plates hang next to a vintage oak mirror from Antique & Artisan. OPPOSITE: The high-gloss bar shines in a deep aubergine from Farrow & Ball.

ELMER BISCHOFF
THE PRADO
PORT

Spaces need to take cues from the architecture—the bones of a home can tell you what it needs, the trick is learning how to listen.

The most formal room in the home, the living room, offsets English roll arms and tufted slipper chairs with charm. A Rose Tarlow stripe ensconces the space, coming off as inviting, rather than imposing; a vintage game table (found at a local antique shop) whose age shows gracefully, also lends a welcoming tone. Communicating with the living room through a set of double doors, the den, cozy in all its emerald-green grasscloth glory, flips the script by using the color palette of the light and bright space on the other side in a different way. A deep velvet sofa, a custom kilim in chocolate brown, sky blue, and pine, and a vintage suzani pillow meld with geometric details like French Aptware to create a cozy space perfect for rainy day reading or a family movie night.

Contrast is the key to this house: East Coast elevated meets the West's laid-back luxe, and saturated hues are balanced by softer shades. Sometimes the best projects are a paradox—and in this case, pairing the unexpected made for a house that's pretty, yes, but also true to its owners' story.

PREVIOUS PAGES AND OPPOSITE: Rust and sage mingle with hunter green and camel in the kitchen/breakfast room. A plaster chandelier above the vintage breakfast table provides hefty scale; handmade chairs by O&G Studio offer contrast. We layered two textiles, a pattern on the roman shades and a textured solid on the drapery panels, to add a warm, spicy note to the mostly white kitchen.

OPPOSITE AND ABOVE: The client's office presented an opportunity to go wild with color. She fell in love with a marigold silk velvet in our fabric library, and we based the room around that sample. A large-scale pattern on the windows captures attention, while a burgundy floral on the sconce shades and sofa pillows punctuates the peach. Stripes in varying shades of orange, plum, and pink bring cheer.

A NOTE ON PRIMARY BEDROOMS

- Primary bedrooms should be serene retreats from the outside world.
- Create zones in a bedroom; a primary bedroom often has more space to allow for additional areas. Two chairs or a chaise work nicely to create a reading nook, while a beautiful vanity desk and chair designate a space for quiet work.
- Serenity is the goal in a bedroom, but that doesn't mean you can't incorporate pattern or color. Infuse small hints via lampshades, pillows, or a patterned kantha at the foot of the bed.

PREVIOUS PAGES: The primary suite walks the line between serene and layered with beautiful Indian block prints and solid textured grasscloth going up the vaulted ceiling, my personal favorite trick to make a room feel cozier and bigger at the same time. OPPOSITE AND THIS PAGE: A botanical textile in spicy reds on the pleated lampshade and throw pillow contrasts beautifully with the sage striped window treatments. A set of vintage botanicals found at auction and matted on green tie the color palette together. FOLLOWING PAGES: A guest room beckons with layers of pattern and color. Wallpapering the ceiling in a small scale makes it feel cozy and calm. PAGES 124–25: To remind the clients of their time spent living in Jackson Hole, in the nursery we incorporated Western elements, such as layered rugs, the artwork above the crib, and a patchwork quilt.

A NOTE ON MIXING PATTERNS

- Start with the palette, then look for patterns in that pre-established color family.
- Begin with one main print (think a botanical chintz or a large geometric) then add a solid or two with a mix of varying textures; checks, stripes, and small-scale patterns like block prints are great complementary patterns.
- Use color as your guide: incorporate different hues from your core colors in the room, allowing the palette to tie the different shapes together into a cohesive story.

Stanley

A BIRD FOR GOOD LUCK

Some houses, empty as they may be, brim with unrealized potential. Such was the case for one that we designed for a young family in New Canaan, Connecticut. The house was a beautiful new build that lacked the charm and character it deserved. It had great bones, however, and both the client and I were eager to dive in.

This gleaming white center hall colonial with handsome architectural detailing is nestled next door to a horse farm where visitors can reach over a weathered wooden fence to feed carrots to retired thoroughbreds. The house is thoughtfully sited amid the splendor of the Connecticut countryside and offers a view of rolling hills from almost every window; it is also close to the town's charming and walkable center.

Classics never go out of style: handsome brown furniture, beautiful botanicals, and handcrafted objects are always a winning trio.

New Canaan reminds me of the area where I grew up outside of Philadelphia, where equestrian farms and leafy trees abound—and I felt confident we could bring the comfortable formality of a traditional home, updated for today's hectic lifestyle, to this locale.

When this family first approached us, I was pregnant with my second daughter and the clients' second son was due to arrive at the same time. I approached the project from the lens of what young families need to live both beautifully and functionally—a question I was simultaneously attempting to answer for myself. Young families are our core clientele, and I form a special bond with clients when we're in the same life stage—we're figuring things out together.

The starting point for this home was the wife's love of nature. She absolutely adores flora and fauna and wanted the home to reflect her affinity for birds, flowers, and botanicals, while not veering into territory that felt too sweet or too themed. We took inspiration from the tiny carved wooden birds that she collects and perches atop door casings for good luck, and set to work on the floor plan. We begin each project by creating a floor plan that we use as a map, giving us

OPPOSITE: A rich antique mahogany sideboard contrasts beautifully with Lewis & Wood wallpaper and a creamy Christopher Spitzmiller lamp. Vintage ornithology prints are a nod to the client's love of birds, flora, and fauna. The gilded sunburst mirror, a favorite tool of mine to bounce light around a room, adds a golden flourish to the formal dining room.

CAROLYNE ROEHM

Dining rooms need to be able to adapt for gatherings both intimate and grand. Additional seating provides flexibility and should look pretty when not in use.

clear direction for intended use of space, and flow. Once the floor plan is set, we color it in with textiles, carpeting, wallpaper, and more—my favorite part of the process.

Intended use of space is the driving force behind our floor plans. I always want to know how clients envision themselves living in each room. Do they foresee entertaining a lot, enjoying movie nights with their kids, hanging out with their dogs on the sofa? Which pieces of furniture need to be corner-free to ensure that littles don't bump their heads, and which can be a bit more geared toward the grown-ups? Here, a picture of an active, gregarious household immediately emerged. The family mentioned hosting big Thanksgiving meals and lively dinners—and I set to work imagining a backdrop for those occasions that could also remain smartly functional for their family life.

For this project, we conceived an overall palette of creams, greens, and blues to anchor the home cohesively and

PREVIOUS PAGES: A formal living room is light and airy with tight-backed English roll arm sofas in creamy linen and fluffy chintz pillows. The sage green and cream window treatments bring the outside greenery in. RIGHT: A vintage French bench sits by the window, providing extra seating for large parties.

The family room is welcoming and comfortable. Green window treatments in a textile by Schuyler Samperton and a custom chocolate brown Moroccan rug anchor the space. A mix of greens, browns, and blues evokes the palette of the outdoors.

CITRUS FRUITS
AMERICA THE INGENIOUS

A NOTE ON TEXTURE

- Try to incorporate a mix of finishes in every room: soft, matte, shiny, cerused, ridged, and pearlized are all examples. The contrast between materials—a tight linen on the sofa, a nubby, fluffy woven rug underfoot—creates interesting tension.
- The eye likes to travel, so spread items across the room to allow them to breathe. Pair opposing textures for a balanced approach.
- On these pages, a variety of accents, like spiral green lamps and a handmade bone inlay drinks table from India, provide texture.

CKREY

ABOVE: Shiplap walls are interesting without feeling loud, and the built-ins allow for a patterned performance cushion, plus cubbies to house totes, wellies, and all the everyday essentials of a busy family. OPPOSITE: The kitchen incorporates the owner's love of blue and white via Urban Electric powder blue pendants, a Delft stripe on the window, and performance ticking on the stools.

Something as simple as hanging plates on a wall can transform a space from boring to brilliant.

lend a natural touch. For bursts of energy in the kids' spaces, we added deep blues, reds, and greens as accent colors. We mixed more formal silhouettes, like a tight back English roll arm sofa, with less formal materials, like sisal rugs and linen upholstery, to strike a balance between polished and approachable. The dining room, one of the most formal spaces in the house, is ensconced in a rich, crewel-like Lewis & Wood floral wallpaper, yet the fanciful detail is tempered by a simple antique cerused-oak mirror that shows its years with patina. I liken this formula to a crisp button-down shirt with the top three buttons undone—the spaces are put together and classic, but not too fussy.

Some projects stick with us long after we've completed the install, and this was one of them. This house was a great lesson in not judging a book by its cover, to look beyond first impressions to understand what the house really could be. It was also a great lesson in the power of letting your imagination run a bit wild, quite literally, courtesy of the natural world just outside the door.

OPPOSITE: The breakfast nook ties the kitchen palette together with a blue-and-white chinoiserie fabric on the chairs. A vintage mahogany round table can expand to seat more when needed. Antique blue-and-white china plates, hung on the wall, continue the theme and frame the doorway leading into the family room in an interesting pattern.

The primary bedroom is a relaxing oasis. We continued the pale blue grasscloth wallcovering all the way up the vaulted ceiling, creating an optical illusion that makes the room seem larger. Framed botanicals flanking the gilded mirror above the fireplace have a similar effect. A variety of patterns play on the bed, but the anchors—walls, carpet, and upholstery—are quiet and soft.

hillea millefolium. L.
Alchemilla Vulgaris. L.

A NOTE ON QUIET SPACES

- Calming spaces need not be devoid of pattern. Walls, floor, and upholstery feel soothing as solids with varied texture. Think: a tight textured silk grasscloth on the walls and a fluffy, nubby wool carpet paired with fine merino upholstery. These variations in textures provide interest while keeping the space relaxed.
- Add pattern in small doses with bedding, pillows, and artwork. Keep windows, lamps, and lampshades solid in soothing hues.

OPPOSITE AND THIS PAGE: Bedding from Matouk (opposite) mingles with Schumacher textiles to create an ikat and botanical marriage. Tiny hints of brass in the framed botanicals and lamp base combine for added warmth and patina. Solid whites in different textures—the linen window treatments and the eggshell-like ceramic lamp base—layer nicely together. A vintage suzani turned into a pillow (right) adds intrigue to an otherwise solid linen armchair.

JACK

OPPOSITE AND THIS PAGE: One of my favorite boy's rooms we've ever done. Red, white, and blue in classic motifs: stripes, block prints, and a beautiful Ralph Lauren cotton dhurrie layered on top of a plush navy carpet. Using the same fabric for the walls and windows creates a cozy, ensconced feeling. The robot artwork and embroidered pillows from Chelsea Textiles add personality.

P
L

A
Y

A NOTE ON LARGE-SCALE PRINTS

- Let the large scale be the star of the show, whether as window treatments or a piece of upholstery. Pair it with solids and small-scale patterns for cushions, chairs, and more.
- In a room where the wallpaper is the main attraction, choose solid hues for the carpet and sofa that draw from the paper. Pillows add punch, but pull from the palette to blend in without feeling loud.
- If a textile is the main event, on upholstery or windows, let a solid textured wallpaper enable the fabric to sing.

PREVIOUS PAGES: A favorite playroom is all fun and games with animal print wallpaper and cushions in happy prints and colorways. ABOVE AND LEFT: In this home's guest bedrooms, large-scale embroidered textiles are the loudest players, and smaller prints complement them via lampshades and bedding. OPPOSITE: The nursery is calming yet fun, with a green-and-white Schumacher embroidered animal print anchoring the scheme. We wanted each boy's room to have its own theme, and the green and blue palette differentiated this room from the red, white, and blue room on pages 146–47. Doubling down on the animal theme, a rattan giraffe head and chartreuse wool tiger area rug add personality.

ABOVE AND OPPOSITE: Outdoor entertaining is easy breezy with two different block printed Indian textiles layered together; mix-and-match Ginori china and green splatterware complete the bohemian vibe. Bamboo folding chairs are a favorite for informal entertaining (plus they look great with every type of table). Sticking to a palette (i.e., pinks and greens) lets the imagination run wild on textiles and place settings.

AN ENGLISH HOUSE IN AMERICA

One of my favorite experiences is working on a ground-up build. Getting into the weeds on everything down to the door hinges is the ultimate exercise in figuring out what a client wants—the more granular the better. For this particular project, we were lucky enough to be paired with the wonderful John Lyons of Lyons McConnell, an architecture and build firm based in the horse country of New Jersey. The collaboration marked the beginning of a long relationship between our firms.

A grand room doesn't have to feel overly decorated; lean into comfortable upholstery and relaxed finishes to create a welcoming retreat.

When these clients first came to us, they were working with an empty plot of land and grand ideas. The wife's mother hails from England, and she had many memories of visiting her mother's side of the family there. Home to her was deeply rooted in the unfussy yet still elegant designs of traditional English country houses, so the clients wanted their home to feel like a classic country estate. They came prepared with a vast array of inspiration photos, and we hit the ground running.

We tried to incorporate their penchant for country style into the little details in the house, working together on selecting stair balusters and window shapes in line with historical references and bringing the beauty of the outdoors indoors—a hallmark of country seats. The windows let in the beautiful natural surroundings from almost every room, so we wove in natural palettes across the entire home to draw attention to the greens, blues, browns, and creams in the pool, the lawn, and the wooden gates of the horse farms nearby.

Early on, the clients learned they were expecting twins, a boy and a girl. Creating a gender-neutral space that was sophisticated

OPPOSITE: An elegantly tufted slipper chair sits pretty with a chintz pillow next to a brass faux bois drinks table. Powder blue raw silk curtains bring the drama in this double-height great room, while the grasscloth-upholstered Chippendale cocktail table and oatmeal wool rug keep things relaxed. Blue delphiniums in a vintage stone urn tie the color scheme together.

ENGLISH FURNITURE

Double-height rooms can be tricky. Instead of trying to minimize the windows, mount the drapery as high as possible to add to the sense of unfussy grandeur.

PREVIOUS PAGES: Light oak herringbone floors and a baby-blue door welcome visitors into the airy two-story foyer. The vintage bobbin entry hall table had a previous life in a Welsh pub. RIGHT: A menagerie of patinated Swedish and French antiques mingle with crisp English-style upholstery, brass finishes, and small hints of chinoiserie in the elegant sitting room.

ABOVE: The formal powder room is airy and elegant with a wallpaper from my collection with The Mural Source; the handsome vanity is a repurposed antique case piece. OPPOSITE: The formal dining room feels English in nature with a large brass lantern holding court above a simple table paired with rush chairs. An antique console adds a sense of history, while the fireplace mantel evokes a Cotswolds' country home.

Storage solutions offer an opportunity to convey personal style. Case pieces have personality; this green cabinet's silhouette is heavily influenced by old-school British larders.

enough for the babies to grow into was a fun challenge—and that room is one of my favorites in the house. The mix of sage green and chocolate brown feels just-grown-up-enough while still erring on the side of playful, and the bunny artwork, which the clients commissioned on their own, makes the room sing.

Deciphering how clients actually want to live in their space is the key to how we ultimately make a house a home. As a designer, I delve into their wishes and lay the groundwork for turning them into reality. Case in point: these clients looked forward to hosting big holiday parties with an extra-tall Douglas fir as the star of the show, so we ensured that the double-height formal living room in this house would be tall enough to fit a giant Christmas tree.

One of the dreamiest spaces in this home is the standout kitchen, which we designed in collaboration with Plain English, masterful British cupboard makers who personify the English country house aesthetic. One of the clients had developed into an amateur home baker during the pandemic, and she wanted room to spread out and knead sourdough with her children. The butcher block island offers

PREVIOUS PAGES: A custom Plain English kitchen sings in its simplicity. The island's butcher block surface was chosen specifically for kneading dough and other bread-making tasks. Clean-lined midcentury wood counter stools and plaster pendants add warmth and contrast. OPPOSITE: A custom larder pantry, made in collaboration with Plain English, houses ceramics, spices, and produce near the breakfast table.

The Fear and the Freedom
KEITH LOWE

A home office feels handsome in a monochromatic palette; tone on tone textures make for a sophisticated take on an English study.

space and transmits the idea of the country without feeling kitschy. The modern stone backsplash that matches the counters serves as a clean and crisp counterpart to some of the more folk-heavy elements in the space. The net result? A calming and welcoming environment in which to cook, eat, and host.

We wanted this new-construction home to feel lived in, so we layered patinated items that tell a story, like the worn antique wooden dining table on one side of the kitchen that nestles atop a vintage Moroccan Berber rug placed over a new, custom textured sisal carpet. This project was a great lesson in the importance of incorporating classic details with pieces that have lived a life—and show it—in order to create the feeling of a home that was loved long before it was even in existence.

PREVIOUS PAGES: The family room is rooted in relaxed elegance, with cushy upholstery and a sea of greens to soothe the eye. RIGHT: His study, with custom millwork by Lyons McConnell Architecture, serves double duty as a library.

WHO WATCHETH
COMPROMISED
PETER STRZOK

PREVIOUS PAGES: The primary bedroom evokes a fluffy cloud; creams mingle with pale blues and grays for a quiet, calming space, with a cumulus-inspired Schumacher print on the bed pillows. THIS PAGE: Pretty primary bath and closet details; I love putting fabric inside glass closet doors for an added, unexpected layer. OPPOSITE: The seating area in the primary bedroom: tailored, yet sweet and airy.

Les jum

A NOTE ON NURSERIES

- Choose furniture that will grow with them—cribs that can convert, case pieces that work just as well in grown-up spaces. Look for items that are durable and made with high-quality materials. Babies grow up before you know it, so invest in furniture for the long run.
- Don't be afraid of utilizing patterns. Choose universal shapes like florals or geometrics.
- It's best to add cute items in small doses so they can be easily switched out later down the line. Think: lamps, lampshades, artwork, pillows.

PREVIOUS PAGES, THIS PAGE, AND OPPOSITE:
The bunny artwork, commissioned by the clients for the twins, is one of my favorite things about this room—it's joyful and fun. We created the bespoke wicker scalloped pelmets; I love the way they play off the striped fabric. The chinoiserie wallpaper is sophisticated enough to be in an adult's room, yet when paired with the stripes, gingham, and artwork, it feels just right for a nursery.

OPPOSITE AND THIS PAGE: The mudroom and laundry room embrace green in all shades. In the mudroom, the millwork is painted in Farrow & Ball's Vert de Terre, a sage green that looks smart against the durable workhorse soapstone sink (custom-made from countertop remnants). The laundry room millwork is painted in Farrow & Ball's Breakfast Room Green.

An outdoor space has its own palette already created by nature; play into it and reflect it in the furniture.

A beautiful pool house created in collaboration with Lyons McConnell Architecture draws the eye straight down the pool. The surrounding view is of peaceful grass-covered country hills. Wicker Serena & Lily outdoor furniture draped with blue-and-white striped towels adds spunk. Don't forget to include drinks tables with outdoor seating—everyone needs a place to put their books, sunscreen, and refreshments.

Encyclopedia of
ORGANIC Gardening

BUCOLIC BEAUTY

The goal for any home we design is to showcase the visible imprint of its inhabitants, and in the case of this special project in Pine Plains, New York, every element is representative of my friend Audrey and her family. Audrey is the founder of The Six Bells, an antique and housewares shop in Brooklyn, and she recently opened an inn in upstate New York. Working on this house together started her love affair with antiquing, and it led to her eventually opening the shop a few years after we worked on her home together, which was a beautiful career pivot. The story makes me happy every time I think about this house.

This upstate compound is located on over sixty acres and spread out over three individual structures that, together, comprise six bedrooms, six bathrooms,

The joy of mixing a collection, even if things feel a little mismatched, creates a space that feels wholly original.

and 4,000 square feet. The houses are laid out in a triangular arrangement amid rolling hills, with a beautiful pool and garden in the center. The oldest of the three structures dates to the pre-Civil War era and retains some of its original beams. One of my favorite things about this home is that each space has a different personality, though all relate back to the same general theme. The airy bedroom in the guest barn is light and breezy, while another bedroom is ensconced in Brunschwig & Fils red-and-white toile. Each has its own quirks, in classic country house style.

Audrey grew up visiting her grandparents' place upstate, and it left an indelible impression on her at a young age. When she toured this property in Pine Plains, she fell in love; it reminded her of their house. Pine Plains is in a gorgeous rural

Mismatched chairs, antique Delft tile around the fireplace, and vintage artwork define the welcoming entry space in this beautiful upstate home. The original ceiling beams and fireplace mantel have a quiet elegance.

MAINSTREAMS OF
MODERN

BULFINCH'S MYTHOLOGY
Encyclopedia of ORGANIC Gardening

Find inspiration in your passions: what do you like to collect, and how can you build a home around it?

part of upstate New York, with bucolic sheep farms and side-of-the-road antique shops; it's remote and verdant and the perfect place to create a secluded and peaceful retreat.

Audrey has always loved English and American country style, so we were heavily inspired by English, Scottish, and Welsh country homes, as well as classic Americana—Shaker furniture, Amish craftsmanship, handmade American quilts. We wanted this home to respect its location, its history, and the era when it was built.

The color palette was inspired by country homes across the pond; the Farrow & Ball green on the millwork in the great room and navy Stiffkey Blue in the kitchen both would fit in perfectly in an old home in Surrey or Kent. Sticking to the palette also helped when mixing patterns, so that the combinations felt intentional and not hodgepodge. Incorporating historically accurate patterns, like toiles, ginghams, and checks, keeps the mix on track.

Together, Audrey and I sourced incredible Americana antiques and vintage pieces—Shaker-style reclaimed tables, handwoven chairs that Audrey found in the Amish communities of Pennsylvania, blue-

PREVIOUS PAGES: The former owner of this barn, an English teacher at the Chapin School in Manhattan, amassed this marvelous book collection and sold it along with the house. The client and her family are incredible stewards and have added their own favorite tomes. Their love of reading was inspiration for the great room. OPPOSITE: Woven shaker chairs made by Amish artisans in Pennsylvania found by the client pair with an antique table.

and-white splatter enamelware to add to her abundant collection. Audrey is the definition of a magpie: someone who buys what she loves and with abandon. I adore working with people who already have their own collections, because nothing feels more unstudied and authentic from a design perspective.

The living room is vast, so anchoring it with a large, comfortable sofa by the fire where family members can sit and read was a room-defining decision. Painting the millwork green transformed the space, and layering in different textiles in the form of cushions, throws, and quilts, paired with antiques from all over, makes it feel curated but not fussy. The library is the heart of the space—a living, breathing part of the house that makes an impact.

Audrey is fearless when it comes to mixing and matching. She buys what she likes and finds space for it after the fact, which is the mark of a true collector. That method makes this home feel genuinely cozy and lived-in. One of the best takeaways from this project was to embrace the unstudied and the deeply personal. As the old Billy Baldwin saying goes, "Be faithful to your own taste because nothing you really like is ever out of style."

The kitchen, with its original beams, nods to the Delft fireplace surround in the foyer with its own Delft tile backsplash. The client's blue-and-white splatterware collection is displayed top right. Woven wicker Matilda Goad pendants illuminate the island.

Necessities and Temptations
THE DEAN & DELUCA COOKBOOK
THE SILVER PALATE GOOD TIMES COOKBOOK

ABOVE AND OPPOSITE: The guest house gleans patina from exposed beams and white paneled walls. The client's finds create a space that feels collected over time. Playing with scale keeps things interesting: the tall lamp and wicker shade contrast with the lowboy dresser. FOLLOWING PAGES: A guest room is swathed in a toile from Brunschwig & Fils, anchored by an antique bed and mismatched Shaker-style nightstands.

LATENCY
ORACLES OF NOSTRADAMUS
ORACLES OF NOSTRADAMUS

A NOTE ON BOLD COLOR

- Color block primary colors for a standout moment.
- Temper primary colors with muddier, muted neutrals.
- Think of color wheel opposites when choosing which primary colors to use: red and blue, cool versus warm. The contrast makes the colors pop against each other.

THIS PAGE: Designing a friend's house is a joy, and designing their kids' rooms is even more fun. In Audrey's son's room, the hidden jib door filled with books (left) is a top spot for hide and seek. Sometimes colors that you wouldn't expect to go together actually look quite nice when you try them. Tempering the heat of primary blues and reds with brown-and-white gingham sheets keeps this room from feeling too high-contrast.
OPPOSITE: Audrey fell in love with the playful Lake August wallpaper in the nursery (opposite) when it came out, and we were both so excited to use it. The rug and quilt pull from the paper's palette.

PALM BEACH TRELLIS GARDEN

Participating in the Kips Bay Decorator Show House had always been a dream of mine. Since I was a little girl, I had attended the show houses with my mother and would linger on the details in each room. The Palm Beach iteration of the show house is particularly meaningful to me; I have visited Palm Beach every winter since I was born, and my parents moved there full time once I left for college. I felt grateful and honored to give back to the community through the Kips Bay Boys & Girls Club.

I spent weeks digging through the online archives of the Palm Beach Preservation Foundation, and their book on John Volk, the beloved Palm Beach architect, in preparation for designing our space. When we found out we were given the exterior lounge and terrace area—the largest space in the home, clocking in at a cool 2,500 square feet—I was particularly inspired by a photo of latticework that Volk used in the exterior entrance to his apartment. The color of that lattice inspired the color of our pergola and the shapes and design of our latticework.

I also studied historic homes in Palm Beach designed by Maurice Fatio. Since the space was so vast, I wanted to create two distinct areas and give the pergola (which we built from scratch) an indoor feeling even though it was outside. That attention to indoor/outdoor flow was a hallmark of Fatio's work, and was a well of inspiration for our space in the show house.

We went into the show house process a bit unsuspecting, and it turned out to be a wild ride. We had extremely tight deadlines to hit, as is the nature of participating in a show house, and the day before it opened to the public, monsoon Florida rains soaked our space. Despite all this, we transformed the area from a concrete slab into a tropical oasis anchored by a mélange of wicker, iron, and plaster furniture. It was an absolute joy (and challenge!) to pull this off in two months, but we did it, and I'm proud of our entire team for working so hard on it. We could not have done it without all hands on deck.

We built this trellised loggia from scratch. Three days before opening day, there was a torrential rainstorm, and everything started leaking through the (hand-painted) roof. Luckily for us, the Florida heat dried things off quickly. What a roller coaster!

OPPOSITE AND THIS PAGE: I grew up going to Palm Beach every winter, so getting to create my dream Palm Beach loggia was so much fun. I scoured eBay for vintage matchbooks from iconic Palm Beach eateries and housed them in a kitschy ceramic frog from KRB (below right). My favorite was from the now-closed McCarty's. The shell mirror (opposite and right) made by Palm Beach Regency pairs perfectly with the palette.

A TREEHOUSE BY THE SEA

Past the hustle and bustle of Main Street in Southampton, down winding, forested roads, a house nestles among tall pine trees and hidden inlets. Built in 2008 but midcentury inspired, with large glass windows that open onto generous views of greenery on all sides, the home was waiting for a new owner to inject fresh life into it.

An on-the-go set of working parents from Manhattan—one in finance and the other in law—were looking for a respite space for uninterrupted family moments. Set on a two-acre compound with a pool and tennis court, the house offered an idyllic peaceful setting for their young daughter and their soon-to-be-born son to enjoy the outdoors and for all four to spend quality time together. It was the perfect blank canvas.

PASSIONS in PRINT

Hubbard Brook

For a house by the sea, let the palette be inspired by surroundings: sand, sun, surf, and trees.

On our first site visit, we found both the flow and the existing finishes discombobulated. The couple gravitated to contemporary silhouettes and clean lines, almost Californian in feel, with a small dose of color and bohemian pattern peppered in for good measure. Our goal was to create a modern, slightly whimsical home that would feel cohesive: light, open, family-friendly, and personal. Above all, it needed to be calm—a retreat and reprieve from their busy life in the city.

One existing feature that we decided to keep was a pair of atriums flanking the foyer that were planted with bamboo. Initially we weren't sure whether they should stay—they were a bit "out there"—but then we walked through for the first time with the clients, and they mentioned that one of the things that had struck them about the

PREVIOUS PAGES: The entry is warm and welcoming in this beach house with bleached wood, bohemian textiles, cotton and jute rugs, and a bounty of fresh flowers. LEFT: The great room feels clean, contemporary, and free-spirited at the same time.

home was that there were views of trees from almost every window. It reminded them, they said, of a treehouse. We collectively leaned into the idea of a house in the sky, a concept reinforced by the bamboo atriums. The views of lush greenery from almost every vantage point give this home the feel of a hidden oasis tucked away in nature.

In collaboration with general contractor Neal Owen, we kicked off a cosmetic renovation, swapping existing mismatched tiles in the bathrooms for timeless creamy white stones and polished nickel, laying down entirely new bleached oak flooring throughout the house, and swathing the interior envelope in fresh white paint or pale, subtly patterned paper to impart an airy crispness.

The palette, inspired by the Hamptons itself, is informed by its surroundings yet not on-the-nose beachy. There's ice blue, pool blue, and aquamarine; yellow for some sunshine; and green running the gamut from lichen to spruce. But the grounding constant in each room is a textured, nature-inspired neutral—whether in the form of bespoke cerused-wood built-in bars in the dining room or the subtly

The family entertains year-round in this house, so we designed the dining table to accommodate a large crowd. Hollywood at Home dining chairs upholstered in a Peter Dunham ikat anchor the space in an arresting pattern. A vintage Indian textile becomes a tablecloth. The Christian Peltenburg-Brechneff watercolor diptych is from KRB.

A happy home is all in the details: here, the multicolor chairs are fun and joyful.

beautiful Nobilis faux bois wallpaper, mimicking wooden paneling, that envelops the primary bedroom.

An eclectic range of textiles and patterns keeps the space feeling fresh, with little pops of surprise. The blue-and-white color scheme in the dining room is traditional, but we made it more free-spirited by layering in an unfussy Peter Dunham ikat and a bold floral artwork by Christian Peltenburg-Brechneff that we found at KRB in New York. And the formal living room explores the full spectrum of colors used throughout the home, but that lively palette is offset by a base of creamy, textured textiles to maintain a sense of zen.

My favorite thing about this project is that the clients, who have since welcomed a third child, use the house year-round, on all the major holidays and during relaxing summer breaks. It's become a gathering place where they create new memories. Our goal for the design was to conjure a sense of inviting effortlessness, a forever summer—and it seems, happily, that we succeeded.

OPPOSITE: We had fun with the breakfast nook, alternating chairs in different colors—a happy scene in a happy house. The blue-and-white dhurrie catches stray crumbs from the kids, while the yellow and green pillows on the built-in banquette tie the chairs to the palette. Unlined woven wood roman blinds filter sunlight without blocking it entirely.

IN THE LIGHT OF NAPLES

PREVIOUS PAGES: The primary bedroom emulates a treehouse with Nobilis faux bois wallpaper. A sinuous textured wool and wood chair peeks out from the corner; Hellenic hand-thrown lamps provide contrast. OPPOSITE: The primary bathroom is crisp and clean with shiplap and honed Carrara marble. ABOVE: Pretty window treatments in a Lisa Fine block print frame the soaking tub.

ABOVE: The daughter's bedroom has twin custom beds for sleepovers and a bright rainbow rug.
OPPOSITE: The son's nursery is ensconced in a textured Phillip Jeffries striped wallpaper that evokes men's suiting fabric. A vintage Oushak keeps the space from feeling too childish.
FOLLOWING PAGES: The outdoor area is set for guests with lemonade and block printed linens.

THE COLOR MONSTER
Counting with a Ladybug

THE BIG MOVE

On March 12, 2020, my husband and I packed up our six-month-old daughter and our dog and left our tiny Upper East Side apartment to book it to my husband's parents' home in Westchester. The city was in a panic—the pandemic had just started—and we thought we'd be back in a week or two. Weeks turned into months, and by May 2020, we decided to let our lease end and make the big move, jumping ship from the city permanently.

Nothing adds more character to a home than a library collected over time. Meaningful objects styled in the bookshelves make it personal.

Our house came to us by pure luck. A family friend knew of a house that was being rented and whose owners might be interested in selling. On a beautiful spring day, we toured it and fell in love with the house and the neighborhood (five minutes from my husband's entire family!). A twenty-plus-year-old home, it needed love, but its bones were great. The millwork was beautiful, the kitchen needed a minimal face lift (new backsplash, countertops), and though the walls of the entire house were covered in a beat up beige wallpaper, a new paint job would be easy enough. My husband and I walked out of the house, and before we even got into the car, we looked at each other and said, "We're doing this."

Over the first two years, we chipped away at the work slowly but surely. With time, the house came together and began to feel like a representation of us—and one that is always evolving. The custom Gracie panels in our family room, the most used room in our home, were a gift from my husband to me for my thirtieth birthday. The bamboo chairs, which we found in Palm Beach at Circa Who while visiting my parents, now serve as pillars for my daughters' fort building.

PREVIOUS PAGES: Fenimore wallpaper from my collection with The Mural Source is a special element in my dining room; I designed it specifically for this space. OPPOSITE: Our sitting room, which we use as a library, is layered with books, collected objects, and sentimental items like the blue Murano vase on the mantel that my mother gave us as an anniversary gift and the Lladró figurines from my grandmother's collection, which she gave us as a wedding gift.

Incorporating items from childhood allows a room to be sentimental; reinventing items from the past in new ways is one of the most satisfying parts of decorating.

This is my favorite room in our house. I found the faux tortoise cabinet at auction for a steal; it was the best deal I've ever gotten! The Nantucket baskets sitting atop the cabinet are from the house where I grew up. A vintage green-and-blue suzani protects the sofa from our dog, Charlie—it's his favorite room, too.

Lee Radziwill

ABOVE: The inside of this cabinet may be better than the outside. I love those silly monkeys! Lena gave me the blue and white watercolor on the top shelf when we finished her West Village apartment. OPPOSITE: A rattan chair from Kenian sits in front of a vintage Baker side table.

The house features an amalgamation of sentimental things I've kept over the years, from my massive collection of interior design books, both vintage and new, to a bronze horse sculpture that always lived in my father's office, to the Lladró figurines my grandmother gifted us for our wedding. Framed lithographs from the house where I grew up—saved for over ten years in a storage unit by my mother, who insisted I would want them one day (she was right, as she always is)—grace the walls.

Almost six years after we moved in, this house still feels special to me every single day. Each time I walk down the stairs and see those lithographs hung exactly as they were alongside the stairs of my childhood home, I am flooded with happy memories. This collection of objects reflects our history, one that we can use to tell our daughters about where they come from, and the houses that came before.

When I set out to design a new space, I think a lot about sense of place, a concept I learned by reading Gil Schafer's books. My most vivid memories are of the homes I grew up in and places I spent time in as a child—and now, with a home of our own and our own children, we're creating those kinds of memories for our girls, for them to cherish one day, too.

OPPOSITE: A custom cotton rug inspired by Bunny Mellon's iconic painted floors anchors the dining room. Vintage Swedish chairs contrast with the dark custom mahogany dining table, an antique reproduction. The lacquered ceiling in pale blue was done by our talented friends at NYC Fine Finishes and is one of my favorite details in our home.

The mudroom is often the most utilized space in a home; give it the love and attention it deserves and it will make you smile every time you open the door.

PREVIOUS PAGES: The breakfast nook is fun, functional, and highly trafficked. Performance Sister Parish cushions on wicker Serena & Lily chairs have seen a lot of sticky fingers and pasta sauce. RIGHT: Our mudroom, one of the happiest spaces in our home. The millwork is Breakfast Room Green by Farrow & Ball. The lampshades are from Bunny Williams Home. FOLLOWING PAGES: Our family room, where the artwork is personal: the Gracie panels were a gift from my husband for my thirtieth birthday, and the lithographs are from my childhood home.

PREVIOUS PAGES: The vintage Moroccan rug from King's House anchors our primary bedroom. Farrow & Ball's Skylight extends the color of the grasscloth wallpaper up to the ceiling, creating a serene feeling. ABOVE: The tufted Serena & Lily bed and custom matching sconce shades and bedding add pattern. OPPOSITE: Our bathroom, a serene refuge.

A NOTE ON MAKING MEMORIES

- These rooms are the most precious spaces I've ever designed. My girls' bedrooms reflect them: bold and sweet, pretty and playful.
- The greatest joy in designing our home was knowing that we were creating spaces for my daughters to make memories in. I hope they always remember the chinoiserie wallpaper with the butterflies and birds dancing in the sky and the pretty little multicolored Oushak at the foot of the bed. Memory is tied up in a sense of place, and I hope these rooms give them just that.

OPPOSITE AND RIGHT: I created this dreamy chinoiserie wallpaper with The Mural Source for my daughter's room. The background color is a sweet, milky pink and looks beautiful when the sun streams in through the woven romans. ABOVE: In my younger daughter's bathroom, a Sister Parish fabric makes a great shower curtain and plays nicely with the block printed Serena & Lily wallpaper.

ABOVE AND OPPOSITE: In my younger daughter's nursery, a beautiful warm peachy-pink silk grasscloth from Serena & Lily sets a calming tone. The glider, covered in a Serena & Lily botanical print, is incredibly comfortable. The monogrammed pillow was a baby gift from my best friends. The woven wood roman shades and white linen drapery panels are both blackout lined, helping to facilitate a good night's rest for all!

VIA PARIGI
5

A NOTE ON OUTDOOR SPACES

- The best outdoor spaces feel like they could exist indoors.
- Utilize a range of materials, including wicker and teak. (Not everything needs to be PVC to be indestructible.) These will patina nicely and give a residential feel to your exterior spaces.
- Cultivate greenery! Growing something, even in a tiny container garden, is deeply gratifying—and the result looks beautiful. (It's also really fun to do with kids.)
- Create different zones depending on your intended use of space: dining, resting, reading, potting. Let the usage inform your floor plan.

PREVIOUS PAGES: The sunroom is one of my favorite rooms in the house. It's outfitted with an amalgamation of items both inherited, like the wooden coffee table from my husband's parents, and found, like the vintage rocker discovered during a late-night Etsy scroll. ABOVE: The raised garden bed, a gift from my mother-in-law when we moved in, is filled every season with new plants and herbs. LEFT: A teak table ages nicely in the sun. OPPOSITE: A Serena & Lily wicker sectional creates space to lounge, read, and entertain on our deck. The tasseled white umbrella, also from Serena & Lily, provides shade on hot summer days.

ACKNOWLEDGMENTS

I am forever grateful to Charles Miers and Rizzoli for the incredible opportunity to share our firm's work in such a meaningful and thoughtful way; thank you from the bottom of my heart. Writing this book was an experience I will always cherish.

The homes in these pages would not exist without the hard work and enthusiasm of the Ariel Okin Interiors team. I am the luckiest to get to work with a group of women as dedicated, bright, and funny as they are. To Laura Whittaker, my left brain, right hand, and work sister for the last decade, I'm so proud of what AOI has become; you are such an integral part of it all. There are no words to describe this wild ride! To Jenn Smith and Victoria Arnoux, our superhuman project managers, you make the wheels turn and give it your all. A huge thank you to Elizabeth Olsen, Lindsey Owen, Ellie Richard, and Kim Kjellman, the talented and creative designers who worked on the projects shown in this book. I appreciate you all immensely. To Catelyn di Leva, I am so grateful for your kindness, positivity, and can-do spirit. We are so lucky to have you!

To Jill Cohen, thank you for your mentorship and friendship—you are the reason this book happened! To Christina Cattarini, who has helped craft our PR strategy from day one, you are truly the best. To Melissa Powell, thank you for your honest advice and sharp eye. To Kathleen Jayes, thank you for your expert edits, making sense of my (extremely long!) first drafts, and helping me to distill ideas into a real book. To Doug Turshen and Steve Turner, thank you for making this look exactly like what I dreamed it could be. You are all so talented, and I've learned so much from each of you.

To the vendors, artisans, photographers, and stylists, we work with, thank you. A huge thank you to Anthony Amiano, Matt Cafiero of MCI Paper, Ciaran Cassidy of NYC Fine Finishes, Mike Ceretta of Ceretta Builders, Helen Crowther, Donna Dotan, Claud Fatu of Fatu Inc. Construction, Jody Finglas of NYC Fine Finishes, Andrew Francus of C&M Shade, Colin Jones of Sisal Rugs Direct, Brian Kanter of Kanter's Carpet, Julie Leffell, John Lyons of Lyons McConnell Architecture, Read McKendree, Maxx Rapaport of Rapaport Wood Flooring, Monika and Artur Sibiga of Kaiser Decor, Christopher Spitzmiller and team, Studio Nectar, Mieke ten Have, and the countless other talented creatives with whom we work every day. We couldn't do any of this without you.

And most importantly, thank you to my family. Ben, you believed in me when I wasn't sure if I could start a business. You are the best husband, father, and friend anyone could dream of—I am grateful every single day that you're mine. I love you to the moon and back. To Mom, Dad, and Bubby, thank you for always making me feel loved and like I can do anything I set my mind to. I am who I am because of you! To Bob and Sue, thank you for being the best cheerleaders and always being so supportive! And to S + A, my favorite people—you are my everything. I learn from you and laugh with you every day, and I am proud of you always. I love you more forever and ever!

First published in the United States of America in 2026 by
Rizzoli International Publications, Inc.
49 West 27th Street
New York, NY 10001
www.rizzoliusa.com

Foreword by Lena Dunham

All photography by Donna Dotan except:
Page 9: Alberto Zanetti
Pages 21, 35, 38-47, 184-199: Julie Leffell
Pages 49-71, 126-153: Read McKendree/JBSA
Pages 200-205: Carmel Brantley
Endpapers: Sameera Print in Blue/Indigo, courtesy of Oscar de la Renta x Lee Jofa

Publisher: Charles Miers
Senior Editor: Kathleen Jayes
Design: Doug Turshen with Steve Turner
Production Manager: Rebecca Ambrose
Managing Editor: Lynn Scrabis

Developed in collaboration with Jill Cohen and Associates, at Sandow Capital, LLC dba JCA

ISBN: 978-0-8478-7633-4
Library of Congress Control Number: 2025946771

Printed in China
2026 2027 2028 2029 / 10 9 8 7 6 5 4 3 2

The authorized representative in the EU for product safety and compliance is
Mondadori Libri S.p.A., via Gian Battista Vico 42, Milan, Italy, 20123,
www.mondadori.it

Visit us online:
Instagram: @RizzoliBooks
Facebook.com/RizzoliNewYork
Youtube.com/user/RizzoliNY

THE MEDICI

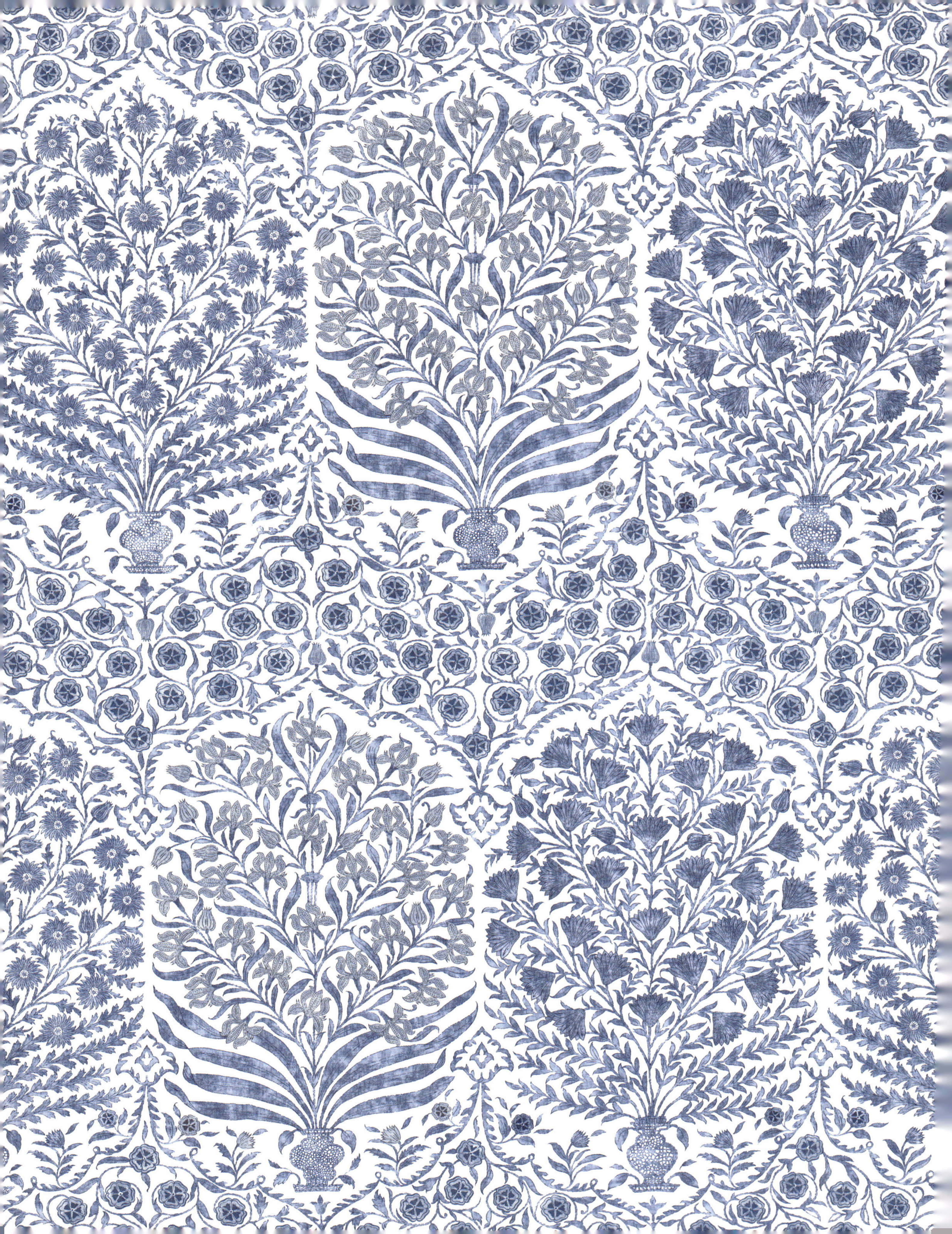